Shapes Everywhere

Shapes in Food

Oona Gaarder-Juntti

Consulting Editor, Diane Craig, M.A./Reading Specialist

A Division of ABDO

ABDO
Publishing Company

visit us at www.abdopublishing.com

Published by ABDO Publishing Company, a division of ABDO, P.O. Box 398166, Minneapolis, Minnesota 55439.
Copyright © 2014 by Abdo Consulting Group, Inc. International copyrights reserved in all countries. No part of
this book may be reproduced in any form without written permission from the publisher. Super SandCastle™ is a
trademark and logo of ABDO Publishing Company.

Printed in the United States of America, North Mankato, Minnesota
062013
092013

 PRINTED ON RECYCLED PAPER

Editor: Liz Salzmann
Content Developer: Nancy Tuminelly
Cover and Interior Design and Production: Oona Gaarder-Juntti, Mighty Media, Inc.
Photo Credits: Ablestock.com, Brand X Pictures, Comstock, Creatas Images, Hemera Technologies, Jupiterimages,
PhotoObjects.net, Shutterstock, Stockbyte, Thinkstock

Library of Congress Cataloging-in-Publication Data
Gaarder-Juntti, Oona, 1979-
  Shapes in food / Oona Gaarder-Juntti.
     p. cm. -- (Shapes everywhere)
  ISBN 978-1-61783-413-4
  1. Shapes--Juvenile literature. 2. Food--Juvenile literature. I. Title.
  QA445.5.G335 2012
  516'.15--dc23
                              2011051113

Super SandCastle™ books are created by a team of professional educators, reading specialists, and content
developers around five essential components—phonemic awareness, phonics, vocabulary, text comprehension, and
fluency—to assist young readers as they develop reading skills and strategies and increase their general knowledge.
All books are written, reviewed, and leveled for guided reading, early reading intervention, and Accelerated Reader®
programs for use in shared, guided, and independent reading and writing activities to support a balanced approach to
literacy instruction.

Table of Contents

Shapes Are Everywhere

Shapes are everywhere in food! Here are some shapes you might see. Let's learn more about shapes.

2-D or 3-D?

2-Dimensional Shapes

Some shapes are two-dimensional, or 2-D. A 2-D shape is flat. You can draw it on a piece of paper.

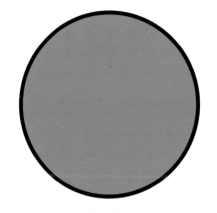

circle
2-D shape

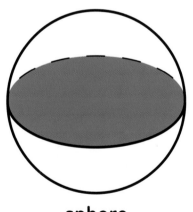

sphere
3-D shape

3-Dimensional Shapes

Some shapes are three-dimensional, or 3-D. A 3-D shape takes up space. You can hold a 3-D shape in your hands.

SQUARE

The **waffle** has many squares. Dennis loves waffles for breakfast. His dad makes them on Saturdays.

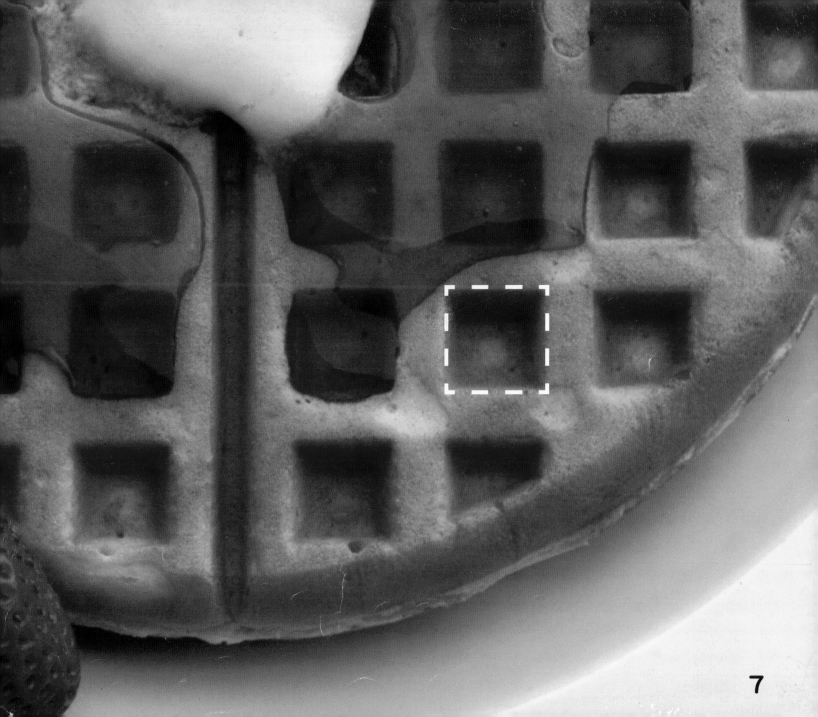

7

CUBE

The cheese is cut into cubes. It is on Owen's **salad**. He is eating it for lunch. The salad also has **olives**, **tomatoes**, and **cucumbers**.

DIAMOND

The blueberry **tart** has diamonds on it. Sam's grandmother baked it. A blueberry tart is Sam's favorite treat.

CIRCLE

The cookies are circles. Grace and her friend cover them with **frosting** and sprinkles.

SPHERE

A gum ball is a sphere. Lily wanted an orange gum ball. But a red one came out of the machine.

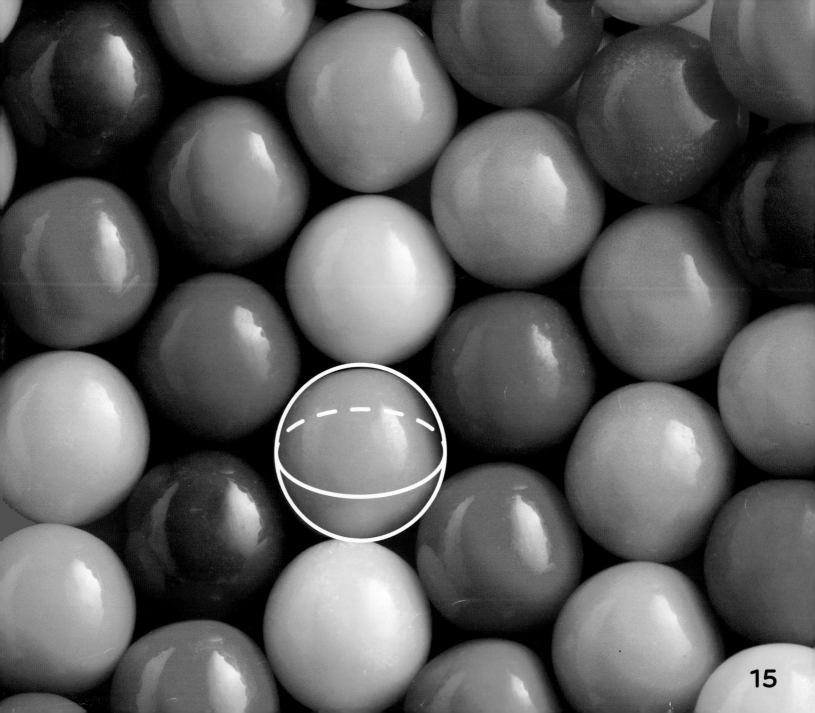

CYLINDER

The glass is a cylinder. Sophia drinks orange juice for breakfast. She eats eggs and a banana too.

TRIANGLE

The pizza is cut into triangles.
Amelia got a good report card.
So she got to decide what to have
for dinner. She picked pizza!

HEART

Some of the chocolates are hearts. Noah buys a box of chocolates. He will give them to his mother for Valentine's Day.

Shapes!

Here are the shapes in this book, plus a few more.
Look for them when you are cooking or eating!

diamond

rectangle

pentagon

hexagon

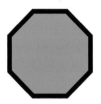
octagon

square

star

heart

oval

triangle

circle

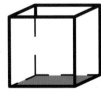
cube

sphere

cylinder

cone

pyramid

How Many?

How many shapes can you find in this picture?

Glossary

cucumber – a long, green vegetable that is often put on sandwiches and salads.

frosting – a sweet coating that is put on cakes and cookies.

olive – a small, oval fruit that can be green or black.

salad – a mixture of raw vegetables usually served with a dressing.

tart – a small pie that usually has fruit in it.

tomato – a soft, red fruit that is eaten as a vegetable. It can be eaten raw or cooked.

waffle – a breakfast food made by putting batter in a special pan with two sides that press together.